My Name is Mercy

Martin Figura

To the staff, patients, and families
of Salisbury District Hospital.

To the NHS

 Fair Acre Press

First published in Great Britain in 2021 by Fair Acre Press
www.fairacrepress.co.uk

Copyright © Martin Figura 2021

The right of Martin Figura to be identified as the author of this work has been asserted by him in accordance with the Copyright, Designs and Patents Act of 1988. All rights reserved.

A CIP catalogue record for this book is available from the British Library

ISBN 978-1-911048-72-5

Typeset by Nadia Kingsley

Cover design by Martin Figura

Cover photo by Monaya Abel

Thank you to everyone who made this project happen. I am especially grateful to those who gave me their time to be interviewed. The lasting impact of the pandemic on their lives was palpable and deeply affecting. I hope the poems go some way towards honouring the experiences and sacrifice of the staff, those they cared for and their loved ones.

Many thanks, Martin

This work is dedicated to the team at Salisbury District Hospital and the whole of the NHS who, when their communities most needed their help, didn't let them down.

Thanks to Dave Roberts and Scott Swinton for their tireless efforts making this project a reality and Stacey Hunter for her support.

"Very impressed. Some poems are really moving, others insightful and others quite haunting. For those of us who have marvelled at the depth of care that the NHS has given to so many, this anthology gives a glimpse of what life (and death) is like behind the headlines. The Salisbury Hospital League of Friends has been really pleased and proud to be part of this important work."

David Stratton Chair of League of Friends

Contents

5.	On Being Interviewed by a Poet
7.	Morning
8.	My Name is Mercy
9.	Protection
10.	Notes Left Behind for a Newbie
12.	Masks
13.	Night Shift
14.	For The Best
15.	The Ridge Line
16.	Praises and a Curse
17.	Space
18.	Mother's Day
19.	To The Shore
20.	Thirteen Ways of Looking at Covid
22.	What is This Place and is it Home?
23.	Here
24.	Fever
25.	A Sonnet for Blood
26.	Heart
27.	The Parish of Odstock
28.	Success in the Time of COVID-19
30.	Screen Sonnet
31.	Stayin' Alive
32.	Life
34.	The Fifth Season
35.	The Birth of Ethan, Christmas Morning

On Being Interviewed by a Poet

How was it for you, this past year, was it:

river swimming in lead diving-boots
or walking in snow, blizzard blind,
was it the Mojave Desert with an
empty map, was it a cumbersome
suitcase and a broken lock, was it
line-dancing in purple crocs, a flock
of sea gulls at a chip shop bin, was it
windowless and continuous, a mouthful
of salt, was it burning car tyres, pliers
and teeth, was it blood dripped into milk,
an alien abduction from a New Forest
glade, sackcloth, shackles, ashes and shale,
was it a skeleton clock, a pickaxe, a mule,
a gilded mirror in flames, was it déjà vu
after déjà vu, was it Nova Scotia in fall,
an abandoned mineshaft in Wales, was it
Easter lilies left to rot, bloodhounds barking
in a parking lot, was it a cold metal bridle?

Tell me in your own words was it difficult,
are you exhausted, what are your hopes,
what do you do to unwind?

Morning

The clock radio wakes me to the news:
infections continue to rise at an alarming rate.
How sudden the day. This first hour seethes
like a fuse, hisses my name through its teeth,
harries me on out through the door.
I have Fatboy Slim's *Praise You* in my earbuds.

The city's a film set for a period drama
with no actors or crew; the cathedral walls
high and wordless. I run my right hand
along the flint for its little stings and blood.
Although I've never thought of myself
as a believer, I have some questions for God.

On the Avon, a swan drifts from under a willow
into mist, as an empty bus exhales on New Bridge Road.
I cut between the cottagey new-builds of Ancient Way
to The Crescent, then Woodbury Rise.

On lucky mornings, a black cat coolly escorts me
across his hunting ground to the chalk meadow,
through the bird song of the hawthorn snowy
with May blossom in March.

The iPod shuffles to Hans Zimmer's
Gladiator score as the hospital chimneys
breach the brow of the hill.

My Name is Mercy

Adapted from Coronavirus: On shift in intensive care - BBCNewsnight. Filmed at Salisbury District Hospital.

Morning my darling, my name is Mercy
I'm your nurse for today, how are you?
Today is the nineteenth of January,
the sun is breaking through.

I'm your nurse for today, how are you?
The outlook should be positive,
the sun is breaking through.
Your wife knows you're here, she sends her love.

The outlook should be positive,
you're doing well, you're safe, you're really safe.
Your wife knows you're here, she sends her love.
Would you like us to phone your wife?

You're doing well, you're safe, you're really safe,
if you can hear me, squeeze my hand.
Would you like us to phone your wife?
It is difficult, I understand.

If you can hear me, squeeze my hand.
Today is the nineteenth of January,
it is difficult, I understand.
Morning my darling, my name is Mercy

Protection

Some days are tempest, we've no choice
other than to bend to its resolve.
Umbrellas squall Maternity Hill like broken birds.

In the giddy rarefied air of the Red Zone
we become fearful of our own carcasses:
our diaphragms – tuneless accordions, our faces

run with rain, our cotton gowns darken to pelts
as we soak, heat is our hostage, we speak only
essentials through the wet prickle of our masks.

*

My emptied out uniform sighs to the floor, I
slowly vanish from the mirror to the harmonics
of pouring taps. The slow elemental immersion
stings during the scalding dissolution.

Sometimes what holds us, our bones
and thoughts, is little more than mist.

Notes Left Behind for a Newbie

     Handover is a waterfall,
we bind together as a raft, otherwise
we might drown.

     There are so many
very sick patients, it's alright to struggle
and admit it. Familiarity with palliative care
improves us day by day.

     As a student you could request
patients simulate their level of emotion
on a scale of one to ten. Fear is the most difficult
emotion to calibrate.

     Shifts will fill themselves
with laughter and dismay, sometimes
until it hurts.

     Empathy cannot be learned
by rote and is known to sneak home
with you after a shift and catch you
unawares.

     Human kindness and sleeplessness
are often bedfellows. Stress is a trickster –
it takes on any number of guises.

Look around the room,
it contains several lifelong friends
whose names you don't yet know.

You'll be asked unanswerable questions
not covered in any scenario you can recall; you must
answer them, whether you want to or not.

There are things we can't begin to explain.
Not all answers are clinical. Tell families the kindnesses
bestowed upon their loved ones on their behalf,
it means the world.

Eat well. Running or walking or yoga
or swimming or singing or cycling or refereeing
will unwind you like as not.

Your transition from awkward
to fully-fledged will occur when you're not
even watching – is invisible in any case.

Remember we are a raft.
At any moment you can reach out
for the hand of someone else reaching out.

Masks

To bridge generations
by imagining a patient
as your own dear grandmother.

To recognise distress
in the purl
of their brow.

To present the illusion
of a calm sea.

To soothe
with the muffled
smile of your voice.

To fashion
a singing bluebird
from your hands.

Night Shift

In the blue orbit
    of a night shift

I glimpse myself
    beyond the window

untethered, an astronaut
    adrift from my craft

in the bleary otherness
    of particles and dust.

If I could reach
    through light years

and touch my blue-gloved hand
    out there

in the refracted constellation
    of flickering monitors,

if I could be heard above
    their vital signs

and respiratory hum,
    I would ask me

if the earth is still
    as beautiful as they say.

For The Best

Everyone walks their worries to the forest
with their dogs to bark and throw sticks.
It's hard to know what's for the best.

We delve into the dark of our pockets
for the list of what it is we need to fix.
Everyone walks their worries to the forest.

Some search for down which burrow their eldest
disappeared; others, only for a stone to kick.
It's hard to know what's for the best.

The more cerebral seek an existentialist
to explain who or what flicked the switch?
Everyone walks their worries to the forest.

The competitive, as ever, see it as a test
and wear a rucksack full of bricks.
It's hard to know what's for the best.

How we envy them, our canine illusionists,
their exuberant ignorance, sniffs and licks.
Everyone walks their worries to the forest.
It's hard to know what's for the best.

The Ridge Line

A Bay Dutch Warmblood of over seventeen hands,
a mighty horse, a cherished childhood dream.
Lizzie whispers *Drum Drum* and he pricks his ears.
They have trust in each other, intuitive and physical.
He loves the reach of the grooming brush working
against the broad combe of his back. He doesn't envy
her, her arms, nor her his four strong legs and mane.

The yard is sharp with impatient clattering and shovel
scrapes. When the river mist softens with the sun
and shadows begin their slow easterly creep back
to themselves, Drum has her. Lizzie is strong, knows
there is still unearthed treasure and blame to be
a useless burdensome beast. He easily forgives
her occasional melancholy, carries her way above

the hollows of the valley. The trees acknowledge
in birdsong their trace of breath as they hack
along the ridge line. Lizzie sees this last year to be
just one of the thousands spelt out across the chalk-
marked Vale and Downs in circled stones, barrows
and flint. The hospital watching over its cathedral city,
her own self a speck at a cottage gate, watching her love

walk to the bluebell woods, a penny whistle in her pocket,
the light rising from her, like a flame.

Praises and a Curse

Praise our solitary hour outdoors unusually warm for this time of year, bless bright skies and open air, praise the river, praise the trees, the heath, the parks, the streets and paths, praise the thrush's warning song and bless the crow's raw harmony, bless the meadow's dungy breeze, praise our houses and hours indoors, bless our trackies, jim-jams, dungarees, praise the ones who raise their hands to volunteer however small or ordinary, praise their calls to loneliness their crammed car boots and gifted time, praise those who pack our bags for life with essential items for us, praise the late-night office cleaners of besmirched fluorescent rooms, bless their cloths, their brooms and bless their hoovers and praise those riders who Deliveroo our curries and our pizzas unto us, praise too all the drivers, bless their vans, their trains and all their buses, bless their trousers' shiny arses, praise the curious cleverness of scientists, their antigens and stabilizers, praise the doctors and the nurses, bless their dutiful hours and hours, praise those too behind their office doors, keeping tolls and puzzling through, praise the chaplain, bless his faith all his prayers and careful listening, bless the corridors and their signage, praise the mileage of the porter, bless his trolley's wonky wheel, praise the chefs and stainless steel, bless their Friday fish and chips, bless their salt and their vinegar, bless their spoons and coloured bins, praise everyone who works from home, bless them in their isolation, bless their internet connection, biscuit tins and dining tables, bless them all and all the rest, the lowest paid and most at risk, curse the cost to them of all of this, curse this invisible *this*, curse its shadow, its cruel intent.

Space

the thought of space   outside of this space   or the walls
of my family and house   cannot be faced   the space
between those spaces   is headphones and downward
faced   the news   cannot be faced   Tesco's empty
shelves   cannot be faced   the chattering school drop off
cannot be faced   people wandering carelessly about their
day   cannot be faced   traffic queues for the Jurassic coast
cannot be faced   Facebook   cannot be faced   laughter
as if *anxious* were not a place   cannot be faced   this
fearful place   must most days   be faced   a wine glass
in a darkness   often faced

Mothers' Day
After: Isolation and Human Kindness article by Dr Kate Jenkins

The limits of heal thy self, each deep breath
coughed, the retching blue lit trip,

the slow recognition of one of us
in a Mexican wave of eyebrows.

Five nights ghosted in a side-room –
its masked visitations and gloved touch,

the time it takes to simply ask for a nurse
to hold my hand and talk of home.

The peckish return of appetite,
delicious want, a little mash with gravy

The boundless gratitude for kindness, luck:
this family, these friends, this work.

To The Shore
After Rilke: Let This Darkness Be a Bell Tower

You have come this far, feel how your presence
fits the space around you, here amongst the intensities,
how it comforts the prognostications of their callous edge.

The tide is pledged to her to and fro; is momentarily
gathered as tinnitus furthermost from the lanky pines –
the air flustered with their scent.

However pale and spent the moon may seem,
she has the might to summon the sea and you
the purpose; the quiet strength to meet it.

Thirteen Ways of Looking at COVID-19
After Wallace Stevens: Thirteen Ways of Looking at a Blackbird

I
A distant planet
Freshly discovered,
Beautiful in its way.

II
The fake news.
The leader's insouciant handshakes.
The next slide please.

III
Among twenty shuttered shop fronts,
The only moving thing
Was the eye of a rook.

IV
A shadowed doorway,
A turned-up collar,
Smoke, a lazy eye.

V
The asset manager surveys
Relinquished city streets
Their windblown banknotes.

VI
Hail, fire, thunder, lice,
Pestilence, locusts, flies,
Frogs, boils and blood.

VII
A grey sea-mine, unmoored
Under a microscope
On a glassy boating lake.

VIII
Human,
New-born
And aghast.

IX
A phial of blood carries your barcode.
A carousel of multitudes –
Parameters' quickening pluck of claws.

X
Rooms as aquariums:
Their mute visited windows,
Kinesics of loss.

XI
Sunday in a suburban cul-de-sac:
The car vacuum's plangent hum,
The jackdaws cracked requiem.

XII
An ultra-fine blade
Taken to the candle wax
Of the space-time-continuum.

XIII
The river curves,
Sifts its sediment
Beyond our grasp.

What is This Place And is it Home?

I couldn't bring my whole self, I needed space in my suitcase for sadness and loss. I climbed the airplane steps in a warm breeze, descended a few hours later, as I knew I would into cold pandemic rain. I watched this place through the fogged window of a hotel room's TV set and acquired a fondness for Norman Wisdom. Candice called from the hospital most days between Rip-Off Britain and Bargain Hunt. We fashioned an idea of this place from experience and expectation. I learned where real food might be found and in which hairdresser's window, I might see myself after quarantine. FaceTime calls are a comfort, my screen crowded with back home faces. I've no answers to their questions just yet. During shifts, I ask those who've been here all their lives what this place is normally like and with each passing day they seem less sure. We work this common ground and familiarity grows with our wonderings.

Here

I came from there to here twenty years past
and long ago paid my dues in the study hours
spent in the pallid company of a desk lamp.

I'm proud to be a part of the arched back
of a twelve-hour shift that cared for whoever
needed it. I earn my place on the bus home.

My ten-year-old daughter was born in this hospital.
Today, she was told to go home where she came from
by someone who felt no need of a mask.

I promise her, one day, she will see people like us
amongst the gilt-framed portraits of dignitaries
on the staircase walls of this city's grand halls.

Fever

The bedroom curtains shiver
in the draught. My head is hot
and full of bees. I'm tucked in
ever so tight and can't separate
bee talk from the quick thrum
of my pulse. What is it they're saying?
Are you cold? I'm cold. The garden
is all around the damp bed and fallen
to autumn. Who are all those squeaking
creatures: their phosphorescent eyes
flashing out from the curtains' blooms?
I'm sure they weren't here last evening.
I hope they don't come any closer,
I can't bear to be touched right now.
In the morning I will ask for them
to be removed. You must excuse me
while I sing myself to sleep.

A Sonnet for Blood
For Pathology

My brother, my mother, my sister
and husband work at the hospital too,
it's in our blood. I need never meet you
to know you are fascinating and particular,
venous and arterial. In blood I discover
your essence, the nitty gritty of who
you are. We take so little, a few
drops, jewels, to tell us the matter.

I'm only interested in continuation,
which way your numbers will
tip. I endeavour not to see through to
your life beyond the cold calculations,
how you have lived, will live still,
who you love, who loves you.

Heart

Our hearts are divided either side
of the septum. A marching band
tattoo of pipes and drums:

right atrium left atrium
right ventricle left ventricle.

The old love songs the clarinettist plays
in the atrium, are irresistible to our
compulsive hearts; they flutter there
like swing doors, the squeals of supply
trollies scuffing down corridors take up
the rhythm. The cardiologist's Doozy
caffeine shots kicks in; *Total Eclipse
of the Heart* indelibly looped in her brain
a fibrillation for the rest of the day.

Salisbury Cathedral's organ is divided either side
of the Quire (with a Q): to the north the Solo
and Great, to the south the Choir and the Swell.
It bellows its chest, fills the nave with notes
where centuries ago, the Bishop of Old Sarum's
arrow stopped the heart of a deer. In atonement
thereafter, a glorious spire petitions the sky.

The Magna Carta and St Osmund look on
as volunteers marshal multitudes into the flow.
Vaccine needles break skin to the tick
of the world's oldest clock.

The Parish of Odstock
For Chaplain John Detain & team

Too modest to blow his own bagpipes around
the wards he leaves them at home, for which everyone
is truly grateful. By his own admission, and like
Bob Dylan, he never *plays a tune the same way twice.*

He knows the hospital very well and his years
as a radiographer have given him (excuse the pun)
a good deal of insight. He takes his lead from the patient
or we may as well pack up and go home.

Many who don't believe in God still ask
for a prayer. There are cards to read out loud
and patient listening as someone summons the breath
to tell you slowly, they know they're dying.
I sometimes have to say, you might be right.

Even churchgoers may lose vocabulary, but not
the longing. It can be lonely here. He is here for that
and for the emptying out of anger or bedpans
and clean sheets. This has been his privilege to bear.
Maybe once a year someone will tell me to go away.

His mask looks as if it could protect him from fire.
He's witnessed the best of us: strangers in bays
finding common cause and strength in their stories:
he's witnessed others speak up for those who can't.
It's important we hold tight to that.

Success in the Time of Covid

In the beginning there was Christmas, a *Great
British Christmas* with all the trimmings. Covid
was far, far away and although we were sad
for those distant people, we still managed to have
a joyful time of it knowing it wouldn't make it
this far, while those in the know readied themselves
for the inevitable while our jolly leader reassuringly
shook hands with everyone. Soon our own hands

were cracked and sore from the washing and
washing. We paid through the nose for sanitiser
and masks. People were fighting in the aisles
for toilet rolls and some of us died.
We all stayed home, and hope turned to prayer.
On Thursday evenings we stood together
but apart, clapping or banging pans with all our hearts.
Our invincible leader became very ill.

More and more of us were catching our breath.
Grief slipped coldly under our doors. Everyone
was anxious and missed loved ones, especially
those who couldn't understand. We craved pasta
and tinned tomatoes. Emboldened wild animals
lolloped through our shopping malls. For one hour
a day we strayed outside to marvel at the sunshine
and bright birdsong. We grew suspicious of each other

and *Zoomed*. Then came the Great British Summer
of defiance, buoyed by military metaphors and *V-Day*
we made sourdough and traffic jams. We fought
it on the beaches, scattering litter and defecating
in the dunes. Yet despite this patriotic fervour
it failed to retreat. We dug in and looked forward
to another *Great British Christmas*. Some who could
afford it, had the foresight to know someone who knew

someone and saw the opportunities; others worked
harder than they ever had for a 3% return and some
were at a loss. The much-heralded *Great British Christmas*
glimmered briefly and as merrily as it could, knowing
the hangover would kick in and blame began pointing
its bony finger about the place. All our difficult questions
were effortlessly rebuffed by saying *vaccine* and *Great
British Success - of which we should be rightly proud.*

An adviser embraced her minister
in delight at the thought of *Freedom Day.*
We, or most of us, rolled up our sleeves
and waited; what else could we do?

Screen Sonnet

Kith and kin corralled glitter-eyed
in latticework for her very final note.
In the end, it didn't seem remote
not being right there at her side.
Her playlist most carefully compiled –
matriarch to the very end – even mute
she brought us close, a screenshot
of occasion for a road well-travelled.

Each day now begins when the dark screen
awakes, we vanish as she appears.
It cares about me and asks the question
we can't turn off – *see more memories?*
and we don't resist and she's there again
and again, still again down the years.

Stayin' Alive

Cardiac arrest is common in critical Covid patients.
The likelihood of recovery is reduced. We've practiced
the art of resuscitation until it's muscle memory:
the heel of one hand pushes the breastbone
firmly down with the Bee Gees in mind.

Covid spreads by respiratory droplets in close contact.
When a heart has stopped, urgency is crucial.
We've practiced the art of donning Level Three PPE
until it's second nature. It's a brutal undignified assault.
Ribs will often break and that's fine if there's a chance
to bring a person back. Otherwise, it's futile and not how

anyone would wish to die, laid out and surrounded,
with their bed clothes stripped off as we try to get needles
in veins and jolt back them to life – it is only human
to spare them this. Kindness isn't always easy.
The privilege falls to us, to give them time for their goodbyes
and then hold their hand as they let go.

Life
From interviewing Hannah McClean, End of Life Team

When it began, my baby was four months old
and I felt extreme guilt at not being there.
The mental conflict is absolute, should I
be leaving my baby and coming back
a few months into maternity leave?

> Anxiety tilting the cradle back
> and forth, back and forth. Vocation:
> a lodestone behind your ribs.

Retired people have said a similar thing.
You need an End of Life Team. The team
is about to be hit by a storm. I came back
in October, a month before the second wave.
I was terrified to drink in the hospital at first.

> The kettle whistling on the hob,
> the *congratulations* flowers brittle,
> their circle of petals swept away.

We covered seven days a week
with a palliative team and felt
really useful, like we were making
a difference. There was much more
of a sense, we are ready for this.

> Oh God, how do they, how
> do other people, you know,
> how do they, how do they.

I think people felt the second wave
wouldn't get this high, nowhere near
as high, four times as high. It was going to be
a slower rise, then like a table top, perhaps
a bit longer before it subsided. They didn't realise.

> The burden of a ship's cargo lashed
> in the hold against the weather's
> capricious mood swings.

It was a Saturday, the sixteenth, we had
seven deaths. I walked onto the ward just
as a patient died and I offered to break the news
to the family. Then I moved to the next patient
I was due to see and they'd already died.

> The deep-sea-diver descends a rung
> at a time through the tumultuous surface,
> doesn't let go until utterly submerged.

And I thought, well tomorrow is it going to be
twelve, is it going to be twenty the next day?
We deal with acute grief after acute grief, you finish
one phone call and then you're straight into
the next acute grief situation: the same.

> Salvation emerges like a photograph
> in a darkroom; slowly, drenched in red,
> awaiting the verdict of light.

I held the phone for him as he was saying
when to plant the begonias out and
don't do it too early, and his son said
I'm going to miss you dad
and he said *you can do this.*

The Fifth Season

Austria's ball season is sometimes called the 'fifth season'.
In memory of Tony, who passed away on the 20th December 2020,
with his wife Gwen at his side. Lovers and dancers to the last.

There are days such as this
where the light finds a way
to promise   a doctor   a wish
and for this cold   white   ward
for one   afternoon   to masquerade
as a ballroom   in dazzling   Vienna
and for us all to be beneath chandeliers
in tailcoats   or pearls   and tiaras
and in all this splendour   from an app
on a phone   an orchestra   conjures
the beautiful blue   of the Danube
for the most elegant   of couples
to drift   quietly there   hand in hand
for a precious few hours,   reminiscing
the courtship they waltzed at the end
of the war.   Their romance never waned
never once   missed a step in all of those years.

She whispers   so softly
farewell   for now   my darling:

I love you
I love you
I love you

The Birth of Ethan, Christmas Morning

The rising numbers have not taken Christmas day off.
The Incident Management Team are undone hair
and bleary-eyed, their anxiety clumsily gift-wrapped
in jokes and bonhomie. Domestic backdrops, each
with their own colourful sheen are bubbles paused
in mid-flight: children aquiver at bauble-laden trees,
an elderly parent fathoming their phone, a spouse
daunted by the commands of Nigella or Delia.
All this held still and quiet as snow as the agenda
takes its toll, until the final item: new births.

In someone's kitchen, right on cue
for the birth of Ethan to Charlotte,
Johnny Mathis croons *When a Child is Born*.

It is said of Ethans: Ethan is enduring, Ethan is strong,
Ethan is optimistic and Ethan is resolute. Ethan
is unphased in his tiny Santa hat, unaware of how
everyone is held in the orbit of his gravitational pull,
that he alone has set the day back into motion,
with all its tinsel, cracker jokes and joyful noise.

Lightning Source UK Ltd.
Milton Keynes UK
UKHW020726061221
395139UK00006B/129